POEMS FOR LAS VEGAS

BY 20 KITSAP POETS
EDITED BY RICHARD WALKER

KITSAP PUBLISHING

Poems for Las Vegas
First edition, published 2017

Edited by Richard Walker
Cover layout by Timothy L. Meikle
Front cover artwork by Dave Granlund
Back cover artwork by Dave Granlund
Project organized by Richard Walker

Copyright © 2017, Michelle Bombardier, Kent Chadwick, Jennifer Coates, Cathy Cuenin, Marsha Cutting, John Davis, Neil Doherty, Carol Despeaux Fawcett, Amy K. Genova, Bev Hanson, Jay Inslee, Anne Kundtz, Diane Lee Moser, Nancy Rekow, Aliona Roman, Tamera Roza, Sharon E. Svendsen, Val Trollefsen, Diane Walker, Jeff Wenker

ISBN-13: 978-1-942661-80-1

All rights reserved. No part of this book may be reproduced or transmitted in any form or by any means, electronic or mechanical, including photocopying, recording or by any information storage and retrieval system, without written permission from the author, except for the inclusion of brief quotations in a review.

Kitsap Publishing
Poulsbo, WA 98370
www.KitsapPublishing.com

50-10 9 8 7 6 5 4 3 2

"And even in our sleep
pain that cannot forget
falls drop by drop
upon the heart,
and in our own despair,
against our will,
comes wisdom
through the awful grace of God."

— *Aeschylus (from "Agamemnon," lines 179-183)*

Introduction

On Oct. 1, 2017, a lone gunman in a 32nd floor room of a Las Vegas hotel opened fire on a crowd attending a music festival on the Vegas Strip. Fifty-eight people were killed. Another 527 were injured.

The mass shooting left the nation grasping to understand how such an atrocity could happen. The day after the mass shooting, Kitsap Weekly — with the assistance of poet Nancy Rekow, coordinator of the monthly poetry readings at Poulsbohemian Coffeehouse in Poulsbo, Washington — asked area poets to write some words that might provide some comfort or help readers process the tragedy and horror of Oct. 1. Nineteen poets immediately responded. One poet, Diane Walker, wrote a couplet and a haiku, adding, "But really, there are no words for the ache in our hearts."

There was something poetic about Gov. Jay Inslee's official response to the mass shooting; we took the liberty of presenting a portion of it here as free verse.

All royalties from the sale of this book will go to the National Compassion Fund, established by Clark County, Nevada, and the National Center for Victims of Crime for the collection and distribution of funds to benefit the victims and their families.

These poems were originally published in Kitsap Weekly and on KitsapDailyNews.com, publications of Sound Publishing's Kitsap News Group in Poulsbo, Washington.

Every other page in this book is blank, in hopes that you may be inspired to write your own thoughts.

Thank you for being an important part of this project.

— *Richard Walker, managing editor, Kitsap News Group*

Dedication

This book is dedicated to those who died in the Oct. 1 mass shooting in Las Vegas, Nevada.

Hannah Lassette Ahlers, 34, of Beaumont, California.

Heather Lorraine Alvarado, 35, of Cedar City, Utah

Dorene Anderson, 49, of Anchorage, Alaska

Carrie Rae Barnette, 34, of Riverside, California.

Jack Reginald Beaton, 54, of Bakersfield, California.

Stephen Richard Berger, 44, of Shorewood, Minnesota.

Candice Ryan Bowers, 40, of Garden Grove, California.

Denise Burditus, 50, of Martinburg, West Virginia.

Sandra Casey, 34, of Redondo Beach, California.

Andrea Lee Anna Castilla, 28, of Huntington Beach, California.

Denise Cohen, 58, of Carpinteria, California

Austin William Davis, 29, of Riverside, California

Thomas Day Jr., 44, of Riverside, California.

Christiana Duarte, 22, of Torrance, California.

Stacee Ann Etcheber, 50, of Novato, California.

Brian S. Fraser, 39, of La Palma, California.

Keri Galvan, 31, of Thousand Oaks, California.

Dana Leann Gardner, 52, of Grand Terrace, California.

Angela C. Gomez, 20, of Riverside, California.

Rocio Guillen, 40, of Eastvale, California.

Charleston Hartfield, 34, of Las Vegas, Nevada.

Christopher Hazencomb, 44, of Camarillo, California.

Jennifer Topaz Irvine, 42, of San Diego, California.

Teresa Nicol Kimura, 38, of Placentia, California.

Jessica Klymchuk, 34, of Valleyview, Alberta, Canada

Carly Anne Kreibaum, 33, Sutherland, Ohio

Rhonda M. LeRocque, 42, of Tewksbury, Massachusetts.

Victor L. Link, 55, of Shafter, California.

Jordan McIldoon, 23, of Maple Ridge, British Columbia, Canada

Kelsey Breanne Meadows, 28, of Taft, California.

Calla-Marie Medig, 28, of Edmonton, Alberta, Canada

James Melton, 29, of Big Sandy, Tennessee.

Patricia Mestas, 67, Menifee, California.

Austin Cooper Meyer, 24, of Reno, Nevada.

Adrian Allan Murfitt, 35, of Anchorage, Alaska

Rachael Kathleen Parker, 33, of Manhattan Beach, California.

Jennifer Parks, 36, of Lancaster, California.

Carolyn Lee Parsons, 31, of Bainbridge Island, Washington.

Lisa Marie Patterson, 46, of Lomita, California.

John Joseph Phippen, 56, of Santa Clarita, California.

Melissa V. Ramirez, 26, of Los Angeles, California.

Jordyn N. Rivera, 21, of La Verne, California.

Quinton Robbins, 20, of Henderson, Nevada.

Cameron Robinson, 28, of St. George, Utah.

Tara Ann Roe, 34, of Alberta, Canada.

Lisa Romero-Muniz, 48, of Gallup, New Mexico.

Christopher Louis Roybal, 28, of Aurora, Colorado.

Brett Schwanbeck, 61, Bullhead City, Arizona.

Bailey Schweitzer, 20, of Bakersfield, California.

Laura Anne Shipp, 50, of Las Vegas, Nevada.

Erick Silva, 21, of Las Vegas, Nevada.

Susan Smith, 53, of Simi Valley, California.

Brennan Lee Stewart, 30, of Las Vegas, Nevada.

Derrick Dean Taylor, 56, of Oxnard, California.

Neysa C. Tonks, 46, of Las Vegas, Nevada.

Michelle Vo, 32, of Los Angeles, California.

Kurt Allen Von Tillow, 55, of Cameron Park, California.

William W. Wolfe Jr., 42, of Shippensburg, Pennsylvania.

A Message from the Publisher

Did 58 people die for no reason in Las Vegas on Oct. 1, 2017? Quickly we might say, yes – we can't see an obvious reason for their deaths and the gunman must have been out of his mind to do what he did. It seems to be a random act of terror committed by a confused individual.

This tragic event has prompted authors and public figures from the Northwest to write these poems to express their feelings. We thank all these authors for their contribution and we hope to inspire all generations to listen to each other and to preserve what our wonderful country has achieved since the times of our Founding Fathers. Today, we enjoy maybe the strongest democracy the world has ever seen. This book may provide an emotional foundation to better understand all our fellow citizens, strengthen our democracy, and help unite against all forms of evil.

Our sympathy and love go out to all of those who have been affected by these terrible shootings.

— *Ingemar Anderson and team, Kitsap Publishing*

Table of Contents

What We Will Tell Our Children After Las Vegas?   1
By Michele Bombardier

Think of a face you love   3
By Kent Chadwick

Joker's Court   7
By Jennifer (Jenny) Coates

No Going Back   9
By Cathy Cuenin

Ten Numbers   11
By Marsha Cutting

Jenny Parks, Kindergarten Teacher   15
By John Davis

Externality   19
By Neil Doherty

Envoi   23
By Neil Doherty

In the Ambulance   25
By Carol Despeaux Fawcett

When the world is spinning, I remember   27
By Carol Despeaux Fawcett

Untitled   29
By Amy K. Genova

The ghost man of Mandalay   31
By Bev Hanson

Untitled   33
By Gov. Jay Inslee

When is a water droplet home?   35
By Anne Kundtz

Message from Las Vegas   37
By Diane Lee Moser

That afternoon the war ended   39
By Nancy Rekow

Silence that consumes everything   41
By Aliona Roman

Cards   43
By Tamera Roza

I Wish The Moon   45
By Tamera Roza

I Say Goodbye Too Long   47
By Tamera Roza

About My Feet   51
By Sharon E. Svendsen

Waxing Harvest Moon   53
By Val Tollefson

A couplet   55
By Diane Walker

A haiku   57
By Diane Walker

It doesn't stay there   59
By Jeff Wenker

Poets' Biographies   61

Notes   66

What We Will Tell Our Children After Las Vegas?

By Michele Bombardier

Sometimes the grandmother is not a grandmother but a wolf.
Sometimes the woodsman comes too late.

Sometimes the wolf's hunger is so great,
he eats his own heart, eats until he is nothing

but teeth and snap and rip. Sometimes
fur, bushy tail and an open-mouth smile means pup,

sometimes it doesn't, and you know what can happen.
We can't protect you.

Usually the woodsman comes in time.
Usually the wolf passes the house.

Think of a face you love

By Kent Chadwick

Think of a face you love
    trace its lineaments in your mind,
    the arch of her cheek,
    the curve of his brow,
    how the lips part for a smile,
    purse for a kiss.

Recall the feelings you've seen
    play across the face you love:
    times of surprise,
    moments of pain,
    instances of love —
    looks given in love to you.
    Your face was loved then.
    The face you face daily,
    its wrinkles and worries,
    all the imperfections
    you've catalogued,
    was loved as it was,
    loved for the you within it,
    blessed by that face you love.

– Continued on next page –

Remember when you saw the chin
    of that face you love
    on a stranger in a crowd?
    So similar it surprised you,
    brought that face you love to mind,
    how the hair or eye
    is shared in other faces,
    the lineaments you've loved
    common to many,
    arranged so variously,
    each face like others
    yet uniquely itself,
    whole, and blessed.

For each face you see
    has been loved
    as you've been loved,
    as you love
    that face you love —
    everyone,
    everyone.

Joker's Court

By Jennifer (Jenny) Coates

Shots ring out, nowhere to hide
inside music turned to madness, harmony
to dissonance.

If I were crazy, I could assume the ensuing
talk in Congress of silencers
to enhance a gunman's experience
was fake,

a parody of government,
macabre humor that bites the heart, so close to
truth, but luckily
untrue.

And yet, the Joker's Court here, unlike
Alice in Wonderland, is now real, and
I am not yet crazy.

No Going Back
By Cathy Cuenin

The radiance
of the harvest moon
is harsh
on our anguish
and there is no going back now
yet I want to turn
to earlier
before this full moon
before the tragedy
to change the rules
the program
and layout
the broken window
to sit a while
watch the waxing moon
grow fatter
engage with the shooter
and to chat
no
not chat
to listen
and then
listen some more
Would I have heard?

Ten Numbers

By Marsha Cutting

3,500,000 – 3668 – 1126 – 500 – 30 – 23 – 21 – 3.5 – 3 –1

3,500,000 — the amount of money donated by the NRA to current members of Congress[1]

3668 — the number of a bill in the House of Representatives that would reduce restrictions on silencers and armor piercing ammunition[2]

1226 — the number of miles from Las Vegas to Bainbridge Island, a distance shattered by the pain of one bullet[3]

500 — the number of people (roughly) who were injured in the Las Vegas shooting[4]

30 – the number of people (at least) said to have been guided to safety by a man who was shot in the neck while helping them[5]

23 — the number of guns the shooter in Las Vegas had with him[6]

21 — the number of years since Congress cut funding for the Centers for Disease Control by the amount spent on researching gun violence as a public health issue[7]

3.5 — the percentage by which the price of gun manufacturer Sturn Ruger's stock rose one day after the Las Vegas shooting[8]

– Continued on next page –

3 — the number of hours some people waited in line in Las Vegas to donate blood[9]

1 — the percentage of people with serious mental illness who have perpetrated gun violence against strangers.[10]

This simply does not compute.

[1] Washington Post 10/2/17
[2] Congress.gov
[3] Googlemaps
[4] NBCnews.com, 10/2/17,
[5] metro.co.uk 2017/10/03
[6] NBCnews.com, 10/2/17
[7] LA Times, 6/14/16
[8] USA Today, 10/2/17
[9] NY Times.com, 10/2/17
[10] Washington Post, 5/18/16

Jenny Parks, Kindergarten Teacher

By John Davis

What were her words before the bullets
entered her the way Hitler entered
Prague and bled the city dry?
In mid-song, between the drums and gunshots

and the singer's voice that twanged
like a flanged guitar in the Vegas night,
what were the last words that Jenny spoke?
Were they a fragment or complete sentence

and did her verb soothe like a smile
one that would urge kindergartners
to sit up, fold their hands into steeples,
open and watch all the people?

Please tell me. I am the substitute.
She left no lesson plans.
Her students are waiting
for the announcements

and the morning sing-along. Please tell me.
Ms. Parks will not be at school today.
Or tomorrow. Students will want me
to tell them what she said.

– Continues on next page –

And how do I create a Jenny voice,
one that rattled and laughed
like rain on an aluminum roof?

Externality

Def. An external effect, often unforeseen and unintended, accompanying a process or activity

By Neil Doherty

Who knows the reason that Fred got a gun,
was it protection or was it for fun?
He did not foresee, I will hazard a guess,
he'd snap in that moment of marital stress.

Gun in the cupboard but key in the door,
three-year-old Alice and five-year-old Shaw,
drawing and carefully taking his aim,
playing, pretending — it's only a game.

Three people slain when a man runs amok,
muscular Christian Conservative stock,
blowing through clinic and shooting at will,
deriding abortion and panning the pill.

Fourteen more killed in the west of L.A.
and yet we will read in the paper today
"guns do not kill" (it's recited by rote)—
kindly remember whenever you vote.

– Continues on next page –

Fifty nine more now in Vegas and yet
NRA lackies in Washington fret;
surely, they say, we dishonor this toll
should we even mention gun rights and control.

But ten-year-old Jason, Chicago south side,
nobody asked him how he would decide
and nobody will now, for what it is worth —
shot in the street in a tussle for turf.

Envoi

By Neil Doherty

Happiness, liberty, life, are to be
sacrosanct only to lesser degree,
quite disregarded by setting our sights
on never constraining gun-ownership rights.

In the Ambulance

By Carol Despeaux Fawcett

She lies in deep grass
under a tree of yellow cherries
sweet air of hibiscus
makes her sleepy

a canopy of faces
red lights paint the sky
her heart stops

a stranger leans in
lips sweet and hopeful
as yellow cherries

When the world is spinning, I remember

By Carol Despeaux Fawcett

When the world is spinning, I remember
these are my loves: red wine,
orange cats, the smell of clove cigarettes,
Leonard Cohen's gravelly voice,
words like sibilate and firefly and lovely and valium,
rain like pebbles on my sunroom roof,
or hail the size of Easter eggs, church bells in the morning,
cradling my guitar like a tired friend,
leaning into corners on my motorcycle,
an unquenchable thirst for love and laughter,
a hunger that isn't hunger but a life
reaching back for itself, singing too loudly,
swimming in the ocean,
warm water like lips sliding over my skin,
the water in me searching for the water not in me,
my body like sand consuming the tides.

Untitled

By Amy K. Genova

A gamble of red
Spilled spirits soaring
Opposite of the bet

The ghost man of Mandalay
By Bev Hanson

On a mission of fun my daughter and her husband checked in.
On a mission of death the ghost man checked in on the very same day.

On Floor 33 my daughter and her husband went to their room.
Just below on Floor 32 the ghost man entered his room.

On Floor 33 my daughter and her husband peered out the window.
They saw a festival of happy people.
On Floor 32 the ghost man peered out with the very same view.
He saw a gathering of targets.

At 5 p.m. on that awful day my daughter and her husband left for the airport.
At 5 p.m. on that awful day the ghost man stayed to do what he meant to do.

My daughter and her husband came home.
The ghost man didn't go home,
And neither did so very many.

Why?

Untitled

By Gov. Jay Inslee

Once again, we are mourning the
violent loss of innocent lives
to a man who had access to
weapons no civilian should
have access to.

It's impossible to know how to stop
every act of gun violence,
but I know with my whole being
that our nation's leaders aren't even trying.

— From Gov. Jay Inslee's statement after the Oct. 1 mass shooting

When is a water droplet home?

By Anne Kundtz

When is a water droplet home?

Pelting its beads onto agave's broad leaves
to drip deep into aquifer, to acequia, to ocean
each drop a ballet battement across shallow ponds,
to rise en pointe before settling;

or is a water droplet home
rising in the desert sun, called to hazy blue sky,
cirrus, cumulus, cumulonimbus,
those giant flat-bottomed thunderheads?

Where does a soul find home
when bullets rain down into a neon ocean
of people, once clapping, swaying waves of music —
and now lying flat, trembling, a turbulent sea
as bullets ping across the seats, ricochet through the terror.

Where does a soul find home?
—In the restless aftermath
souls rise above the screams
leave long black bags of hurt and anger
for loved ones and survivors to carry.

Souls gather in thin wisps
as we pick up prickly shards,
as we begin to heal this desert home.

Message from Las Vegas

By Diane Lee Moser

They rained from the sky
no address … . .
mixed messages
from a mixed mind.

Second Amendment
opened the door
insanity stepped through
held bodies in its hand.

Now our Nation cries out
for the innocent,
the broken hearts,
The Future … …

That afternoon the war ended

By Nancy Rekow

That afternoon the war ended
we picked every green tomato in the garden,
dipped them in flour,
fried them for supper,
and nobody
argued over the dishes.

Hours we ran through the sprinkler
leaping like salmon to its wet circular hiss,
shooting each other over and over with the hose,
flopping on the grass, gasping,
air heavy with Mother's peonies.

It was any summer night.
There the big dipper hung.
Up on the porch, dozens of papery moths
blundered against the light
and fell with no sound.

Silence that consumes everything

By Aliona Roman

The world didn't seem to stop to me.
Even as my mother blared CNN from our living room on the second of
October,
I couldn't feel feelings for hours.
Nothing but numbness, while hours before hundreds felt
Confusion and fear.

The world stopped turning for them.
For the mothers and fathers, husbands and wives, brothers and sisters.
It was a bang,
Cut off by screams of concert goers
That were heard throughout the streets of Sin City that night.

The world continued that morning.
It was with silence
That consumes everything.
Numb and still,
My world continued to turn.

Cards

By Tamera Roza

Fates are shuffling
Like a deck of cards
In a Child's hands

Unlit matches
Stacked up against
Gasoline cans

I Wish The Moon
By Tamera Roza

I wish the moon a magnet
Strong enough
To suck the bullets out

I Say Goodbye Too Long

By Tamera Roza

I say goodbye too long
I look them in the eyes and hold on
So tight I break my heart bones
The what ifs are unbearable

What if they don't come home
There is a shooter in the classroom
Firing bullets into our babies

What if they are swallowed
By a hurricane and die choking
My name on their lips

What if they are scorched
Charcoaled into ashes
By wild fire

What if they hang themselves
In the school bathroom
To prove a bully wrong, or right

What if they take or are slipped
A bathroom cabinet pharmaceutical
That gets them high forever

– Continues on next page –

What if they go to hear their favorite
Singer with their favorite friends and
They all get gunned down dancing

What if they don't come home
There is a shooter in the classroom
Firing bullets into our babies

I say goodbye too long
I look them in the eyes and hold on
So tight I break my heart bones
The what ifs are unbearable

About My Feet
By Sharon E. Svendsen

Yes. They're called feet,
metric feet, the accents
in lines of poems.
"Kaboom Kaboom" is two iambic feet.
"Ta ta tum, ta ta tum" is two
anapestic feet.

May my feet walk toward mercy.
May my feet walk toward peace.
May my feet walk toward reason,
reason and truth.

And

May my feet kick away
(in words)
at anger, torture, murder.

May my footprints overflow
to a better world.

Waxing Harvest Moon
By Val Tollefson

Waxing Harvest Moon
Blood red in a smoky sky
Reflecting the lost

A couplet

By Diane Walker

What choice have we, when dealing with such horror and such grief, but to insist that we take steps to end this slaughter?

A haiku
By Diane Walker

Echoes of gunshots
shimmer above the desert;
warblers fall silent.

It doesn't stay there
By Jeff Wenker

Scarlet pillows
Seeping
Hemorrhaging
Spreading

like a stain
Our great stain
nothing removes

Lady MacBeth
has nothing on us

An answer?
Any answer?
Stoicism
Acceptance of pain
and suffering.

Wherever it happens …
it doesn't stay there..

Poets' Biographies

Michelle Bombardier is a Northwest poet whose work has appeared in Atlanta Review, Bellevue Literary Review, Raven Chronicles, Artemis, Fourth River, Poetry International Online and nearly 30 others. Her book, "Leaving Damascus," is a finalist and contender for Write Bloody Press 2017. She earned her MFA in poetry at Pacific University. She works on Bainbridge Island as a speech-language pathologist in her clinic after working in Seattle hospitals. She has lived in Kitsap since 1991 and is developing Fishplate Poetry, an offering of workshops and retreats for poets while raising funds for humanitarian relief.

Kent Chadwick is a poet living on Bainbridge Island. He self-published "God comes to us like a caterpillar: Jesus' stories retold for kids" and "A Balance of Shadows: Gregg Chadwick's Paintings" through Wisdom Press in 2010. His poetry has appeared in Floating Press Review/Pontoon, World Haiku Review, Switched-on Gutenberg, The Raven Chronicles, Left Bank, Sojourners, and the anthologies "Burning the Midnight Oil: Illuminating Words for the Long Night's Journey into Day" and "Deep Down Things: Poems of the Inland Pacific Northwest."

Jennifer (Jenny) Coates moved to Bainbridge Island with her husband Samuel Brody, a classical pianist, and now 17-year-old daughter, Cymbeline Brody, in 2006. She is an international and domestic tax and business lawyer by trade, but has many other interests which round out her days, including writing poetry. She works out of her own law practice, Jenny Coates Law, and likes that her employer gives her time to pursue her diverse interests. Jenny's poems have been published in several anthologies and collections, including "Just a Little More Time" as part of the Grief Dialogues project and as part of the yearly Poetry Corners and Ars Poetica events occurring during National Poetry Month.

Cathy Cuenin is retired from nursing and tug-boating, and now enjoys painting, writing and reflections on soul matters. Her first book, "The Way I Walk, from Tugboat to Transplant," is a moving story of challenge and adventure. A deep relation to the natural world and concerns for social justice are reflected in her prose and poetry.

Marsha Cutting is a semi-retired psychologist from Bainbridge Island who sails, advocates for disability issues, and is involved in anti-racism and environmental work.

John Davis is the author of two collections, "Gigs" and "The Reservist." His work has appeared recently in DMQ Review, Iron Horse Literary Review, One and Rio Grande Review. He teaches high school and performs in blues bands.

Neil Doherty is a retired economics professor from the Wharton School of the University of Pennsylvania. He favors traditional rhyming and metric verse and writes on a variety of subjects, including science (an avid reader) and religion (a skeptic). He lives on Bainbridge Island with his wife Caroline and dog Codie.

Carol Despeaux Fawcett earned her MFA degree from Goddard College. She is an award-winning poet whose work has appeared in many journals. In the Pacific Northwest Writers Contest, her memoir and her poetry have won first place and her current work-in-progress, a fantasy novel, was a finalist. Her poems have been finalists in the Writer's Digest Annual Poetry Competition and the Surrey International Writers' Conference. She received a poetry grant from Return to Creativity and co-writes a blog for writers at OneWildWord.com. She is publishing her first book of poems, "The Dragon and The Dragonfly," later this year. Her website will be www.cdfawcett.com.

Amy K. Genova is a new resident of Poulsbo and has several poems published in a variety of journals.

Bev Hanson's creative outlet focused solely on digital art and photography until she became the coordinator for Ars Poetica (art and poetry combination) in Kitsap County for two years. She became intrigued with the writing portion because she read so many wonderful poems and illustrated some of them. With encouragement from poet and publisher, Nancy Rekow, she ventured to another creative discipline, poetry. Beverly now enjoys the written word besides the illustrative end of creating and loves the challenge. A far departure from her career in finances and tax preparation, she revels in both forms of expression at this time in her life.

Jay Inslee is governor of Washington. He served in the U.S. House of Representatives from 1999-2012, and in the Washington state House of Representatives from 1989-1993. He lives on Bainbridge Island.

Anne Kundtz writes with her students in Creative Writing and sophomore English on Bainbridge Island. Her poems have appeared in Writing All Morning, Ars Poetica, Poetry Corners, Mountain Mail, and other print and online publications.

Diane Lee Moser has written poems all her life, but never shared them until the past two years. She's a mother, grandmother, and great-grandmother. She's been a social worker, crisis counselor, bookkeeper, traveler, and started a food bank and the first B&B on Bainbridge Island. Life experience has been her teacher, she said, and she has now discovered the joy of sharing heartfelt words with others.

Nancy Rekow, a Bainbridge Island resident, is a widely published and award-winning poet. She has taught poetry and creative writing workshops for all ages for more than 40 years. She's also edited, helped design, and published various books, many with her late poet/teacher husband, Everett Thompson. Along the way, she's helped organize and publicize the annual San Carlos Poetry Readings (now in their 34th year); monthly Poulsbohemian Coffeehouse Poetry Readings (now in their 25th year); Ars Poetica, featuring artwork interpreting poems (now in its seventh year) and various other poetic/artistic events.

Aliona Roman is one of Anne Kunitz's Creative Writing students.

Tamera Roza is a Bainbridge Island native and a mother of two children. She has a lifelong passion for poetry in particular, but finds all forms of writing gratifying and cathartic. "In making and sharing art, we heal and grow," she said.

Sharon E. Svendsen's fiction, articles, and more than 200 poems have been published in literary magazines and many other periodicals and anthologies. Her work has most recently been published in Plainsongs, Rat's Ass Review, Feathertale #15 and #16, Spank the Carp, Decasp, Poetry Corners, and Ars Poetica. She has a BA in English with a Creative Writing Emphasis from the University of Washington.

Val Tollefsen is a retired trial lawyer currently completing his term as mayor of Bainbridge Island. He has often found peace and meaning in the poetry of others, and is honored to have made a seventeen syllable contribution to this healing gesture.

Diane Walker is a contemplative photographer, painter, playwright and poet who produces a daily blog of poems and photos (www.facebook.com/contemplativephotography). A former Seattle marketing executive, Walker lives on Bainbridge Island and serves as volunteer station manager for Bainbridge Community Broadcasting.

Jeff Wenker is a writer and winemaker. He worked last year in the Barossa Valley, South Australia, a region featured in his latest novel, "The Russian Books." He studied Russian History at the University of California, Berkeley, and was featured in "When I Was There," a collection of essays and stories about Cal. Recently, he completed a vintage at Siduri Winery in Santa Rosa — a place also traumatized by tragedy — which will be featured in his upcoming novel, "Mad Crush," a work in progress. His other books are available on Amazon. www.amazon.com/Jeff-Wenker/e/B00IQRKU0Y

Notes

www.ingramcontent.com/pod-product-compliance
Lightning Source LLC
Chambersburg PA
CBHW071750080526
44588CB00013B/2203